W9-AYR-583

J   575897
355.8   12.95
Ita
Italia
Weapons of war

DATE DUE			

GREAT RIVER REGIONAL LIBRARY

St. Cloud, Minnesota 56301

WAR IN THE GULF

WEAPONS OF WAR

Written by:
Bob Italia

575897

109835

Published by Abdo & Daughters, 6535 Cecilia Circle, Edina, Minnesota 55439.

Library bound edition distributed by Rockbottom Books, Pentagon Tower, P.O. Box 36036, Minneapolis, Minnesota 55435.

Copyright©1991 by Abdo Consulting Group, Inc., Pentagon Tower, P.O. Box 36036, Minneapolis, Minnesota 55435. International copyrights reserved in all countries. No part of this book may be reproduced in any form without written permission from the publisher. Printed in the United States.

Library of Congress Number: 91-073074   ISBN: 1-56239-027-9

Cover Photo by: Bettmann
Interior Photos by: Bettmann/Department of Defense

Edited by: Rosemary Wallner

TABLE OF CONTENTS

The awful reality of war. The city of Bagdad, Iraq lay in rubble after the U.S. Air Force unleashed its relentless bombing attacks.

INTRODUCTION

On January 16, 1991, the United States and its allies, beginning with a massive air assault, unleashed Operation Desert Storm against Iraqi troops that had invaded the tiny Middle East country of Kuwait. Iraq's leader, Saddam Hussein, thought his troops could withstand the assault. The country had just withstood a brutal eight-year war with its hated neighbor Iran. Hussein was confident that his army—the fourth largest in the world—had enough firepower and battle experience to repel the U.S.

But Iraq had never seen a military force as powerful or sophisticated as America's. In the end, the "Mother of all battles," as Saddam Hussein called it, lasted only six weeks. The reason?

The devastating firepower of America's weapons of war.

MISSILES & BOMBS

The missiles and bombs used in Operation Desert Storm are a lot more complex and powerful than the missiles and bombs used in World War II or the Vietnam War. Most are guided to their targets by high-tech devices— and they strike with deadly accuracy.

- *The TOW Anti-tank Missile*—The TOW (**T**ube launched, **O**ptically tracked, **W**ire-command link guided missile) is a mobile and powerful weapon designed to destroy tanks and other heavy armor. The TOW weighs 47.4 pounds. Its warhead is six inches in diameter and weighs 13 pounds, giving it a lot of armor penetrating power. It has a range of 12,000 feet, can travel up to 625 mph., and its guidance system allows the gunner to guide the missile through smoke, fog and dust. The TOW is usually mounted on high mobility multi-purpose wheeled vehicles (HMMWV or "HumVees").

The TOW Anti-tank Missile is a mobile weapon designed to destroy tanks and other heavy armor.

- *The Hellfire Missile*—The Hellfire missile is larger, heavier, and faster than the TOW. Its warhead is twice as large, and it has incredible destructive power. No armored tank or vehicle in existence can withstand a direct hit from a Hellfire missile.

The Hellfire is usually launched from an Apache attack helicopter. The missile is laser guided. A laser beam is directed at the target and the Hellfire zeros in on the laser energy. The laser can be directed from the attacking helicopter, another helicopter or airplane, or from a ground vehicle. As long as the laser beam is kept on the target, the Hellfire never misses. The Hellfire helped make the ground war a very short and successful campaign because it destroyed many of Iraq's tanks.

- *The Patriot Air Defense Missile*—The Patriot anti-missile missile was also very useful in the Persian Gulf War. It knocked out scores of Iraqi Scud missiles launched at Israel and Saudi Arabia—and saved countless lives. The Patriot is so new, it had never before been used in combat. No one knew for certain if the sophisticated surface-to-air missiles would work. But after the first Scuds were shot out of the sky,

Patriot Missile, the weapon that gave the U.S. the edge.

the Patriot had established itself as a techno-
logical wonder—and earned it the name
Scudbuster.

A Patriot missile weighs 2,200 pounds. It stands
17 feet high, is 16 inches wide, and is mounted
in a group of four on a mobile launcher. It can
travel up to Mach 3 (three times the speed of
sound) and has a range of 43 miles. Its incredible
performance relies on a sophisticated guidance
and control radar that tracks the incoming enemy
missile and directs the Patriot to its target. Each
Patriot Defense System can cover an area of two
square miles.

- *The Scud Missile*—The Soviet-built Scud
  missile quickly became the villain of the
  Persian Gulf War. Iraq used the missiles as
  instruments of terror, aiming them at civilian
  targets in Saudi Arabia and Israel.

The Scud is a surface-to-surface ballistic missile.
(A ballistic missile is one that falls freely to earth
after a self-powered ascent). It can be launched
from fixed sights or from mobile launchers, and
can carry conventional (high explosive), chemical
(gas), biological (germs) or nuclear warheads. The
missile stands 40 feet tall, weighs 22,000
pounds, and can travel 280 miles.

- *The Sparrow and Sidewinder Missiles—*
  The radar-guided Sparrow missile and the
  heat-seeking Sidewinder missile appear on
  most U.S. and Allied aircraft. They are 10 feet
  long and fly twice the speed of sound. Range
  varies from 10 to 25 miles.

Sidewinder missile.

- *HARM Missiles*—The air-to-surface **H**igh-speed **A**nti-**R**adiation **M**issiles (HARM) are used to knock out enemy radar systems. They weigh 807 pounds, stand nearly 14 feet tall, and are 10 inches in diameter. The missile homes in on enemy radar impulses and destroys the systems with a high explosive warhead.

- *The Maverick Missile*—The air-to-surface Maverick comes in two varieties: television-guided and heat-sensitive infrared guided for use at night. With the television-guided variety, the pilot merely selects a target on his television screen, then launches the missile, which locks on to the target. The pilot can then watch the missile on the television screen as it travels to its target.

The supersonic Maverick weighs up to 670 pounds and stands over eight feet tall with a one-foot diameter. It has a range of 25 miles.

AGM-65 Maverick air-to-surface missiles mounted beneath the wing of an F-4E Phantom II aircraft.

A Hawk missile being fired.

- *The Hawk*—This is a medium-range air defense system that can shoot down low- and medium-altitude enemy aircraft. Each radar-guided missile can reach heights of 33,000 feet and can travel more than 19 miles. It comes equipped with a radar system, and there are three missiles to each launcher.

- *The Stinger*—This is a shoulder-fired infrared homing missile that locks onto the heat trail of enemy aircraft. A small motor launches the Stinger. Then when the small missile is far enough away from the gunner, a larger rocket propels the Stinger to its target.

- *Gliding TV-Guided "Smart" Bomb*—The gliding "Smart" bomb, like the Patriot missile, was extremely useful during the Gulf War. Its pin-point precision made it possible to bomb targets without causing civilian deaths.

TV-guided smart bombs come in many sizes. The 2,450-pound version is 13 feet long, 1.5 feet wide and has a wingspan of five feet. It is guided by a television system that locks in on a target while operating the bomb fins that steer the bomb.

- *Laser-Guided Smart Bomb*—Laser-guided bombs home in on a laser beam aimed at the target by the attacking aircraft, another friendly aircraft, or from the ground troops. When the bomb strays from the target, sensors work the bomb fins to return the bomb to its deadly course.

Close-up view of two GBU-12 Laser guided bombs mounted under the wing of an F-4E Phantom II aircraft.

- *Durandal Anti-Runway Bomb*—This bomb is very unique. It is launched about 200 feet over its target at a speed of nearly 700 miles per hour. As it falls, its parachute opens and points it straight down at the runway. Then a rocket fires, driving the powerful warhead 16 inches into the concrete before it explodes.

- *Harpoon Anti-Ship Missile*—The Harpoon is a ship-to-ship missile designed to sink enemy vessels. It uses a radar homing system to find its target. The Harpoon stands nearly 13 feet tall, weighs 1,145 pounds, and is one foot in diameter. It has a range of nearly 60 miles, has a 488-pound high-explosive warhead, and is powered by a 660-pound-thrust jet engine.

- *Tomahawk Cruise Missile*—The launching of Tomahawk cruise missiles from the battleships *Missouri* and *Wisconsin* in the Persian Gulf signaled the beginning of Operation Desert Storm.

These super-fast missiles can be launched from ships or aircraft. They stand nearly 20 feet tall, are 20 inches in diameter, and have a wingspan of nearly nine feet. They are first launched by a solid-fuel booster rocket, then a small turbojet propels them to their target with deadly accuracy.

A United States F-15 Eagle, the best fighter aircraft in the world.

AIR POWER

- *The F-15 Eagle*—The F-15 was designed with one purpose in mind: to give the United States Air Force the best fighter aircraft in the world.

The F-15 is a large fighter. It has a single seat and can carry 68,000 pounds of weapons and fuel. It is powered by two turbofan jet engines that give 47,960 pounds of thrust. The F-15 can travel up to 1,650 miles per hour—2.5 times the speed of sound (Mach 2.5)!—and can fly as high as 65,000 feet. Most other aircraft can only fly as high as 45,000 feet.

The F-15 comes equipped with a 20mm Gatling gun that fires 100 rounds per second. But what makes the F-15 so deadly is its missiles. The F-15 carries four air-to-air Sparrow missiles. The Sparrow is radar guided. It can travel at Mach 4 (four times the speed of sound) and carries an 88 pound high explosive warhead. The F-15 can also carry six deadly Sidewinder missiles.

The pilot of the F-15 rarely sees his target. When his radar detects approaching enemy aircraft, he launches his missiles from miles away.

The missiles lock onto the radar image and strike with deadly accuracy. As the few Iraqi pilots who challenged the F-15s found out, the Eagle rarely fails.

Since most of the Iraqi Air Force refused to engage the F-15s in dog fights (combat between airplanes), the Air Force used the fighter for air-to-ground attacks. The F-15 Strike Eagle, a two-seated version, was fitted with laser guided bombs, cluster bombs, and Maverick missiles. It attacked enemy bunkers, tanks, and other military targets with deadly accuracy.

The Strike Eagle comes equipped with a **L**ow **A**ltitude-**T**argeting for **N**ight (LATN) pod that is mounted on the nose of the plane. This allows the pilot and the weapons system officer of the Strike Eagle to fly and attack at night with great precision.

- *The F-16 Fighting Falcon*—The F-16 was designed for economic reasons. For the price of one F-15, three F-16s can be built. The Air Force wanted to buy many small, quick, and maneuverable aircraft to offset the Soviet Union's huge number of Mig-21 fighters. The F-16 became the answer.

The F-16 is a single-seat fighter powered by a single turbofan engine that produces 23,830 pounds of thrust. The Falcon has a top speed of 1,400 miles per hour (Mach 2). Since it is much smaller than the F-15, the Falcon is much more maneuverable, and is excellent in dog fights.

*The F-16 Falcon can reach speeds of
1,400 miles per hour.*

The F-16 can carry 12,000 pounds of weapons, including four Sidewinder missiles. It also comes equipped with a 20mm Gatling gun that can fire 515 rounds of ammunition. Like the F-15s, the Fighting Falcons were used in Operation Desert Storm mainly for ground attacks.

- *The C-5 Galaxy*—Without the C-5, Operation Desert Shield and Desert Storm would not have been possible. It was responsible for quickly moving most of America's troops and equipment into Saudi Arabia.

The C-5 Galaxy is responsible for moving equipment and troops – it's the best cargo plane in the world.

The C-5 is America's best cargo plane. It is also one of the largest planes in the world. The Galaxy is powered by four turbofan engines that give the huge plane a cruising speed of 515 miles per hour. It has a range of 3,750 miles and can carry an incredible 221,000 pounds of cargo.

The Galaxy has a large nose door. The cargo deck measures 112 feet by 19 feet, allowing the plane to carry everything from troops to tanks—and even helicopters. The Galaxy can take off from and land on unpaved runways.

- *The Fairchild Republic A-10 Thunderbolt (Wart Hog)*—Officially, the A-10 is named the Thunderbolt. But because it is so ugly, pilots call it the "wart hog." The name has stuck. Although it is an ugly plane, the A-10 is beautiful when it comes to performance.

The A-10 was designed specifically for attacking large tank columns. It comes equipped with the most devastating automatic cannon of any attack plane in the world—the General Electric GAU-8/A Avenger. The Avenger is a 30mm Gatling gun. It fires a .78 pound bullet that travels at 3,500 feet *per second!*

The bullet is very heavy by all Gatling gun standards. And the speed at which these bullets travel is remarkable. Even more, each bullet is made of a very dense material (depleted uranium). No armor on earth can withstand its powerful impact. Once each projectile pierces its target, the uranium—heated by the incredible impact—explodes with incredible fury. It showers the inside of the armored vehicle with flaming metal fragments, igniting fuel and detonating ammunition. The A-10 can carry 1,174 rounds of ammunition and can fire at a rate of 2,100 or 4,200 rounds per minute.

The A-10 also comes equipped with Maverick missiles, laser guided bombs, Rockeye anti-armor cluster bombs, Snakeye retarded bombs, anti-personnel cluster bombs, and Hellfire missiles.

The A-10, which weighs 20 tons, is powered by two turbofan engines that produce only 9,065 pounds of thrust each. The plane's top speed is only 425 miles per hour. That makes it very vulnerable to enemy anti-aircraft fire. To counter this threat, the A-10 is fitted with some very special features.

The cockpit is surrounded by titanium able to
withstand a 23mm shell. The fuel tanks have
a special foam that plugs leaks. If necessary,
the A-10 can return to its base powered by only
one engine.

Though it is ugly and slow, the A-10 Thunderbolt
remains one of the most lethal weapons in the
U.S. arsenal.

- *The Lockheed F-117 Stealth Fighter*—Of all the techno-weapons used in Operation Desert Storm, none can compare in design or complexity to the F-117 Stealth Fighter.

The F-117 was designed specifically to avoid detection by enemy radar. Because of its odd shape and construction materials, the black F-117 can either deflect or absorb radar energy so that very little impulse returns to the radar operator. The F-117 also carries its fuel tanks and weapons internally where radar energy can't detect them. And the engines do not give off an afterburn (exhaust or heat) which can also lead to detection. All of this makes the F-117 "invisible" to the enemy. It can then deliver its deadly cargo of bombs—especially at night—without being detected.

The F-117 carries laser-guided bombs. It does not have a Gatling gun or any missiles. These would make the plane more vulnerable to radar detection. When you fly a black jet at night that can't be detected by radar, you don't have much need for defensive weapons.

The F-117 is powered by two General Electric engines that produce 12,000 pounds of thrust each. Much of the information about the F-117 is still classified (top secret). Since the United States is the only country that has a stealth fighter, it wants to keep this information from other nations who might want to develop their own stealth fighters. The F-117 was one of the first planes to bomb Iraq when Operation Desert Storm was unleashed.

- *The F-111 Aardvark*—The F-111 was the first aircraft to use "swingwing" technology. When taking off and landing, the wings would be positioned forward. When attaining top speed, the wings would be swept back. The swing-wings also gave the F-111 the ability to perform as a fighter (wings swept back for speed and maneuverability) or a bomber (wings swept forward to carry heavier payloads and travel long distances).

The two-seat F-111 is equipped with two turbo-fan engines that produce 25,100 pound of thrust each. The aircraft can reach a speed of 1,653 miles per hour (Mach 2.5). It also has an active **E**lectronic **C**ounter**M**easures (ECM) system that can jam enemy radar, and an imaging infrared (FLIR) system that allows the plane to attack at night with laser-guided bombs. The F-111 is also big enough to carry nuclear bombs. It has a 20mm Gatling gun, and carries cluster bombs and anti-runway missiles.

Though designed to be a multi-purpose aircraft, the F-111 is used mainly as a bomber. It can carry 30,000 pounds of bombs and has a range of 3,000 miles.

- *The F-4 Phantom "Wild Weasel"*—The F-4 is a very specialized aircraft. It is designed to detect, locate, and destroy enemy missile batteries and radar installations.

For it to be successful, the F-4 comes equipped with a lot of sophisticated electronic equipment. It has a **R**adar **H**oming and **A**ttack **W**arning **S**ystem (RHAWS) and electronic jamming equipment. To knock out the missiles and radar equipment it detects, the F-4 carries HARM missiles that home in on enemy radar impulses. It also carries Sidewinder missiles in the event the aircraft comes across enemy planes. Along with the F-117 Stealth fighter, the F-4 was one of the first aircraft launched against Iraq at the start of Operation Desert Storm. Once most of the enemy radar and missile batteries were destroyed by the F-4s, the Air Force could fly and attack at will with very few casualties.

- *The B-52 Bomber*—There is little high-tech about the B-52. It was built years before many of the pilots in Operation Desert Storm were born. But when it comes to destructive power, nothing in the U.S. Air Force can rival it except for the B-1B bomber.

The B-52 is a huge plane. It is 160 feet long, weighs 490,000 pounds, and has eight turbojet engines that produce 13,750 pounds of thrust each. The B-52 has a top speed of 650 miles per hour and can fly at 50,000 feet and 8,800 miles without refueling.

What's so impressive about the B-52 is its payload. It can carry 12 750-pound bombs under each huge wing and 27 more in its bomb bay. Typically, the B-52 drops its payload from seven miles up.

The aircraft can also carry air-launched cruise missiles with conventional or nuclear warheads, nuclear bombs, and Harpoon anti-ship missiles. The B-52 also has four radar controlled .50 caliber machine guns in its tail turret for air defense.

The B-52 has a crew of six: the pilot, co-pilot, navigator, radar navigator, electronic warfare officer, and a gunner. It comes equipped with sophisticated electronic equipment to help it penetrate enemy air space. To prepare for the ground war, B-52s regularly bombed Iraqi positions along the Saudi Arabian-Kuwaiti border. The relentless and devastating pounding by the B-52s eventually crippled the Iraqi front lines, and made them eager to surrender.

- *The Harrier II*—The Harrier is one of the most unique attack jets of the Navy. Based on a British design, it can take off and land vertically like a helicopter.

The Harrier is powered by a 22,000-pound-thrust engine. It is 47 feet long, and can carry smart bombs, Harpoon and Maverick missiles, and general 2,000 pound bombs. It also comes equipped with a television/laser targeting system.

The Harrier II is a unique attack jet. It can land and take off vertically like a helicopter.

TANKS & GROUND ARMOR

- *The M1A1 Abrams Main Battle Tank*—This tank is the most powerful and complex tank ever built. It is 26 feet long, 12 feet wide, eight feet tall, and weighs 63 tons. Its main weapon is a 120mm laser-guided cannon that can fire armor-piercing shells 2.5 miles away from its target while traveling at 20 miles per hour. The cannon remains locked on the target even when the tank is racing over hilly terrain. The M1A1 also has two M-240 machine guns and one .50-caliber Browning machine gun.

The M1A1 is powered by a 1,500 horsepower gas turbine engine. Its top speed is 42 miles per hour—and it consumes six gallons each mile. Its range is 288 miles. It comes with chemical, biological, and nuclear fallout protection for its four-man crew. The M1A1 also has a laser rangefinder and thermal (heat) viewing for night fighting. Some of the M1A1s are fitted with reactive armor that explodes outward when hit by enemy fire. This deflects the force of the explosion away from the tank crew. The M1A1 tanks led the charge into Kuwait and Iraq when the ground war began.

- *The M-60 Main Battle Tank*—This four-man tank is equipped with a 105mm cannon, an M-73 machine gun, and a .50-caliber machine gun. It is powered by a 750-horsepower engine that produces a top speed of 30 mph. Its range is 298 miles. The M-60 weighs 60 tons. It is 23 feet long, 12 feet wide, and 11 feet tall.

- *The **M**ultiple **L**aunch **R**ocket **S**ystem (MLRS)*—This three-man weapon system fires 13-foot-long, 9-inch-wide rockets that are mounted in two six-missile cannisters on a self-propelled launcher. Each missile weighs 600 pounds and can travel more than 18 miles. All 12 missiles can be launched in less than 60 seconds, and can spread up to 8,000 bomblets over a 400 yard area. The missile launcher has a top speed of 40 miles per hour.

- *The M198 Howitzer*—This is a stationary cannon that is hauled by truck. It is the finest artillery piece in the Army. It fires a 155mm shell up to 24,059 yards through a 20-foot barrel. The entire cannon is 41 feet long, and requires a crew of 11. These cannons pounded Iraqi positions along the Kuwaiti border at the start of the ground war.

(Above) the M198 Howitzer – a stationary cannon hauled by a truck – it's the finest artillery piece in the Army. (Below) the M-60 Main Battle Tank – it weighs 60 tons and is 23 feet long, 12 feet wide and 11 feet tall.

- *The M109 Howitzer*—This is a self-propelled cannon that looks like an over-sized tank. It has a crew of six, a turret, and a 17-foot barrel that can fire a 155mm shell nearly 20,000 yards. The M109 weighs 28 tons, and its top speed is 33 miles per hour.

- *The Bradley Fighting Vehicle*—This is a tracked, lightly-armored troop carrier. It comes equipped with a two-man turret carrying a 25mm cannon, a machine gun, and TOW missiles.

The 60,000 pound Bradley has a top speed of 38 miles per hour. It can travel through water at a speed of 5 miles per hour. It is 22 feet long, 11 feet wide, and 10 feet high. The Bradley is powered by a 600 horsepower diesel engine and has a range of 300 miles. Reactive armor is also fitted to the Bradley. It has a three-man crew and can carry six infantrymen.

- *Light Armored Vehicle LAV-25*—The LAV is used by the Army and Marines. It has a 25mm cannon and a 7.62mm machine gun. Its most outstanding characteristic is its eight huge tires. The LAV has a top speed of 62 miles per hour on land and seven miles per hour in water. It can easily climb a 60 degree slope.

The LAV is 21 feet long, seven feet wide, eight feet high, and weighs 28,400 pounds. It is operated by a crew of three and can carry four infantrymen.

- *The HMMWV (HumVee)*—The **H**igh **M**obility **M**ulti-Purpose **W**heeled **V**ehicle plays many different roles on the battlefield. It can act as a supply truck, an ambulance, troop carrier or an attack vehicle when mounted with a TOW anti-tank missile.

The four-wheel-drive HumVee weighs nearly two tons. It has a top speed of 65 miles per hour and has a range of 300 miles.

Soldier launches a TOW anti-tank missile mounted on a HMMWV all terrain vehicle.

SEA POWER

- *Battleships*—The U.S. sent two 50-year-old battleships to the Persian Gulf: the *Missouri* and the *Wisconsin.* Each of these "battle-wagons" carried 32 Tomahawk cruise missiles. They have nine 16-inch guns that can hurl 2,700-pound shells 20 miles. These were the guns that pounded Iraqi positions along the Kuwaiti coast. They also have 12 five-inch guns and four Phalanx **C**lose **I**n **W**eapons **S**ystems (CIWS). The Phalanx is a radar-guided Gatling gun that can fire 3,000 rounds of 20mm ammunition per minute at anything that gets through the air defenses.

These battleships weight 57,500 tons loaded and are nearly 900 feet long. They have a top speed of 33 knots, powered by four massive turbine engines that produce a total of 212,000 horsepower that turns the propeller shafts. Their hulls have one-foot-thick armor. They also have a landing deck on their fantails for anti-submarine helicopters. To make it all work, a crew of 1,525 is aboard.

The battleship USS Wisconsin.

- *Aircraft Carriers*—Air support for Operation Desert Storm would not have been possible without these mammoth floating fortresses. Aircraft carriers such as the *Theodore Roosevelt*, the *Midway*, and the *Ranger* have crews of 5,000 or more. Half of them are sailors. The other half are Marine and Navy aviators and mechanics. The ships can carry between 70 and 90 aircraft, depending on their size.

Typically, an aircraft carrier weighs over 90,000 tons. Some, like the *Roosevelt,* are nuclear powered, and can generate 280,000 shaft horsepower to four giant propellers. Carriers can travel up to 30 knots. The deck of a carrier can be over 1,000 feet long and 250 feet wide. They launch their aircraft with steam-driven catapults, and snag the returning craft with a series of reinforced cables that stretch across the deck.

- *Cruisers*—A cruiser like the *USS Bunker Hill* is a much smaller ship than an aircraft carrier or a battleship. It weighs 9,600 tons and is powered by four gas turbine engines, and can travel up to 30 knots. Cruisers are 565 feet long and 55 feet wide. They carry helicopters,

Aircraft carrier USS Midway.

Harpoon missiles, two 5-inch guns, two Phalanx systems and have six torpedo tubes. The main purpose of a cruiser is to protect carriers from enemy submarines, ships and missiles by using their great variety of firepower.

Destroyer USS Moosbrugger.

- *Destroyers*—Destroyers like the *USS Moosbrugger* are the smallest members of the carrier task force. They are 530 feet long, 55 feet wide, and weigh 8,040 tons. They carry eight Harpoon missiles, Tomahawk cruise missiles, 5-inch guns, the Phalanx system, torpedoes, and two anti-submarine helicopters. Because they are small, destroyers can reach a top speed of 34 knots.

- *Guided Missile Destroyers*—Ships like the *USS Wisconsin* are very unique. Most of their weapons are missiles. These guided missile destroyers were designed to shoot down enemy aircraft that try to attack the carrier task force.

Guided missile destroyers carry the Sea Dart missile system, two Phalanx Gatling guns, and a 5-inch gun. They also have a Lynx anti-submarine helicopter. These destroyers weigh 4,775 tons and are powered by gas turbine engines.

- *Minesweepers*—These specialized ships, such as the *USS Samuel B. Roberts*, scour the seas for enemy mines. They are only 225 feet long, 40 feet wide, and weigh 1,315 tons. But they are equipped with the most sophisticated minesweeping devices in the Navy. All minesweepers come with a tethered mine neutralization system. This system has sonar, video, cable cutters, and a detonation device used to destroy enemy mines. Minesweepers have wooden hulls and are covered with fiberglass to fool mines that are triggered by metal. Each minesweeper can travel up to 13.5 knots and has a crew of 74. Many sweepers were used in the Persian Gulf to protect the carrier forces of the Navy. Minesweepers are very effective. And even though their task sounds dangerous, rarely are they damaged by enemy mines.

- *Submarines*—Little is known about the use of submarines in the Persian Gulf War. But they were there, ready to unleash their awesome firepower at a moment's notice. One of the cruise missiles that struck Baghdad was launched from the *USS Louisville*.

Many submarines are nuclear powered and can reach a speed of 30 knots submerged. Typically, they are 360 feet long, 33 feet wide, and weigh 6,900 tons. Each has 12 vertical launch tubes for missiles that can carry conventional or nuclear warheads.

THE GREATEST MILITARY ON EARTH

Before the Persian Gulf War, the United States was unsure of its military might. It had received a humiliating defeat in Vietnam, and its new and expensive weapons had yet to be tested in a real war. But now that the Gulf War is over, the incredible success of these techno-weapons has established the U.S. as the greatest military power on earth.

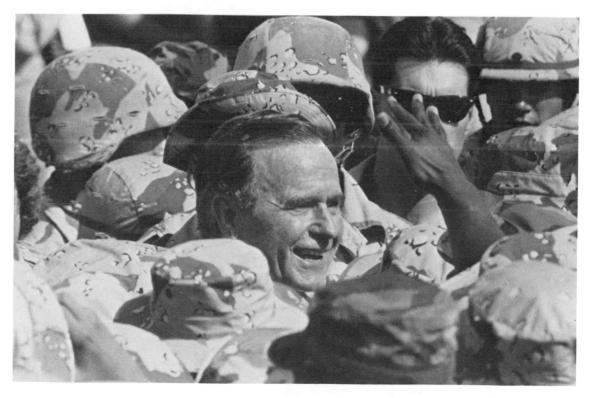

President George Bush congratulates the Marines in the Saudi Arabian desert.

GLOSSARY

ALLIES—Nations who cooperate with each other to fight a common enemy.

ARSENAL—A large stock of weapons.

AVIATOR—A pilot.

BALLISTIC—A missile that falls freely to earth after it is launched.

BOMB BAY—The section of an airplane where bombs are stored.

BOOSTER ROCKET—A separate rocket that launches another rocket.

CATAPULT—A mechanism that launches airplanes from an aircraft carrier.

CONVENTIONAL WARHEAD—A warhead that uses a non-nuclear high explosive.

CROSSHAIRS—The thin lines (vertical and horizontal) on a weapon's sight.

CRUISE MISSILE—A missile that is guided by an internal computer.

DETONATION—To explode a bomb or warhead.

FANTAILS—The "wings" of laser-guided bombs.

GUNNER—The person who shoots a weapon.

INFRARED—An "invisible" light that is created and detected with special equipment.

LAUNCHER—A mechanism used to fire missiles.

MACH—A term used to indicate the speed of sound.

PAYLOAD—A cargo of weapons.

SUPERSONIC—Faster than the speed of sound.

SWINGWING—The mechanical wings of a jet that can move forward and backward.

WARHEAD—The explosive tip of a missile.